Killer Plants

The Venus Flytrap, Strangler Fig, and Other Predatory Plants

By Mycol Doyle, Ph.D.

Illustrations by Allison Atwill

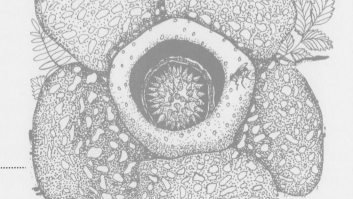

Lowell House Juvenile   Contemporary Books

Los Angeles   Chicago

To Mary, Wolfie, and Terrance—live
long and prosper

Acknowledgments

The author would like to thank Dr. Willem Meijer for providing the rare rafflesia photographs and the Department of Biological Sciences at California State University, Fullerton, for allowing access to their collection of carnivorous plants.

PHOTO CREDITS:
cover photo: Dennis Sheridan
Mycol Doyle: *pg. 8, pg. 9 (inset), pg. 14, pg. 18-19, pg. 20, pg. 21 (inset), pg.24, pg. 25 (insets)*
Joe Mazrimas: *pg. 12, pg. 13 (inset), pg. 26*
Willem Meijer: *pg. 16, pg. 17 (inset)*
Chuck Powell: *pg. 6-7*
Dennis Sheridan: *pg. 4, pg. 5 (inset), pg. 7 (inset), pg. 10-11, pg. 22-23, pg. 23 (inset), pg. 27 (inset), pg. 28-29*

Requests for such permissions should be addressed to:
Lowell House Juvenile
2029 Century Park East, Suite 3290
Los Angeles, CA 90067

Manufactured in the United States of America
ISBN: 1-56565-056-5
Library of Congress Catalog Card Number: 92-40209
10 9 8 7 6 5 4 3 2 1

Have You Ever Seen A . . . Killer Plant?

I never thought that I would see
A plant that could consume a bee,
Or one that causes misery
To such huge objects as a tree!

Unlike animals, most plants have the special ability to make their own food from air, water, minerals, and sunlight. Some plants, however, cannot make their own food, so they must get it by capturing and consuming animals themselves, or by stealing food from other plants. Plants that capture and eat animals are called **carnivorous plants**. **Botanists** (scientists who study plants) are fascinated by these carnivores because they lure their victims into special "death traps," then kill and ultimately digest their animal guests. **Digestion** is the process by which the plants break down or dissolve food into a liquid that can be soaked up by the plant's leaves. Just like spiders, carnivorous plants liquefy the insides of insects by using special digestive chemicals called **enzymes**.

Plants that feed off other plants are known as **parasitic plants** (called **vampire plants**). Like many carnivorous plants, parasitic plants cannot survive on their own. But, instead of turning to the animal world for food, these plants have turned to their closest of kin—other plants! Like the legendary vampire bat, parasitic plants live on their victims' life-giving juices (a mixture of sugar, water, and other nutrients). Once a plant victim has been found, the parasitic plant will spend the rest of its life attached to it, feeding on the host plant's sugary juices. Like all good parasites, the parasitic plant must not go as far as killing the plant that feeds it. To do so would be suicide for the parasite. However, some parasitic plants do weaken their hosts and in the end kill both host and parasite anyway.

Read on and discover thirteen cannibals of the plant world that either eat their prey or leech off other plants in *Killer Plants*!

The Strangler Fig

Tropical forest plants that grow on *other* plants are called epiphytes (*epi* means "upon," and *phyte* means "plant"). Usually, epiphytes do not harm the plants they grow upon, but one epiphyte is a born killer—the strangler fig. Among the tallest and most sinister trees in tropical rain forests, this dangerous plant eventually destroys its host tree by shading and strangling it to death!

Once the strangler fig has killed its host, the dead tree trunk rots away, leaving behind a free-standing strangler fig, composed of a hollow shell of roots and stems. Because the inside of the "trunk" is now hollow, if you wanted to, you could place a ladder *inside* the tree leading to the world's coolest tree house! But you wouldn't want to stay up there too long!

A VERY STRANGE STRANGLER

Time lapse: hundreds of years

Birds feast on strangler fig fruits, then perch on another tree and leave strangler fig seeds behind.

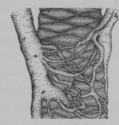

Seeds sprout and form a huge branched root system all along the tree trunk. Each root grips the side of the doomed tree. Then the stem of the strangler fig grows above the leaves of the host plant, where there is light for the strangler fig to grow.

Robbed of its precious food source—the light—the helpless host tree grows weaker and weaker. Now in the shade, and almost entirely constricted by tightly binding roots, the once healthy tree dies.

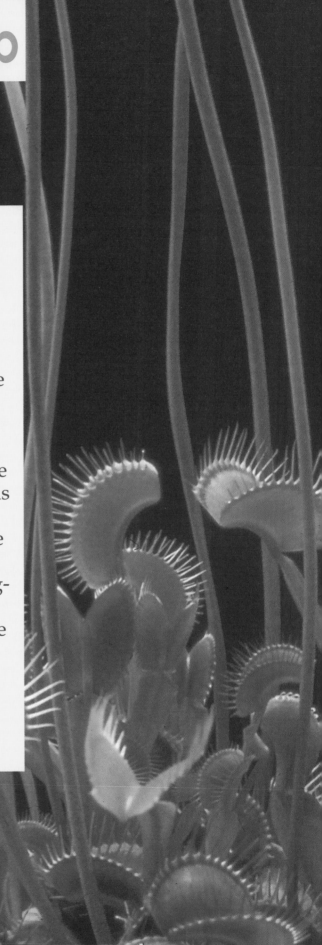

The Venus Flytrap

(*Dionaea muscipula*)

....

location: *eastern United States*

Probably the most famous killer plant is the Venus flytrap. Its snapping trap can catch insects and bugs in an instant! About the size of a dime, the trap looks like a miniature bear trap when it's closed. Small animals, such as insects and spiders, are attracted to the trap because of the dark reddish color inside. The animals also come to the Venus flytrap to smell the sweet-smelling nectar in the "shell" portion of its leaves.

Inside the trap are two rows of "trigger hairs." When the trigger hairs are touched by a passing prey animal, the trap will snap shut and digest the prey. Like a cemetery, the trap keeps its victims' exoskeletons (the hard outer shells of insects) buried within the Venus flytrap.

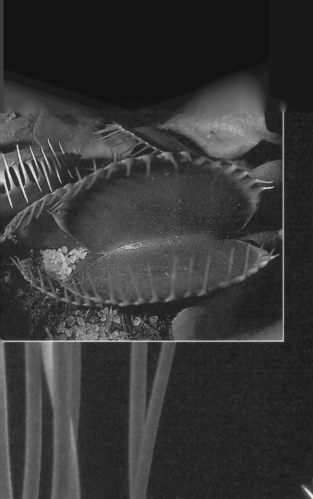

WATCH OUT FOR THE TRAP

Time lapse: 2 to 3 days

Attracted to the nectar, the victim—here a fly—touches off the trigger hairs.

The trap closes very quickly, with the prey animal caught inside.

As it continues to tightly squeeze its prey, the Venus flytrap releases digestive juices that slowly turn the soft parts of the captured animal into liquid.

The liquid "soup" is soaked back into the leaf like a sponge, and the trap opens, ready for another victim.

The Mistletoe

Mistletoes are semi-green plants that are only partly parasitic on many different kinds of trees. They aren't completely dependent on trees because they have chlorophyll, the green pigment that allows them to make some of their own food. But they don't make enough, so they must take the rest of their food from the trees they grow on.

Like most parasitic plants, mistletoes do not have true roots. Instead, they have special organs called haustoria (hahss-TOR-ee-uh), which dig into the victim and ultimately suck its water and sugary juices. While mistletoes may cause serious harm to the many kinds of trees they grow on, one European legend suggests that mistletoe hung over doorways during Christmas brings romance and happiness to those people who pass under them. To host trees, nothing could be further from the truth!

KISS OF DEATH

Time lapse: many years

The fruit of a mistletoe is eaten by a bird.

Within the fruit are very sticky seeds, which stick to the bird's beak. The bird removes the seeds by rubbing its beak against a nearby branch.

Once on a branch, the seeds begin to develop, and soon invade the host tree's tissue. Once inside, the sprouting seeds are able to draw food from their host, allowing the young mistletoes to grow.

The Sundew

(Drosera)

location: *all over the world*

Nearly a hundred different kinds of sundews grow around the world, and they all have one thing in common—they are deadly! While some are only an inch or so across and others are large bushes, they all have special colored leaves that attract small animals, especially flying insects. The leaves are covered with deadly tentaclelike hairs. Each hair is tipped with a shiny drop of sticky fluid that traps the victim.

In feasting on its prey, the sundew leaves behind only the insect parts that couldn't be digested. Look closely at a sundew, and you may find insect exoskeletons scattered in the sticky hairs!

FEASTING ON A BEE

Time lapse: 1 to 2 days

Upon landing on a sundew leaf, an animal becomes stuck to the droplets on the hairs.

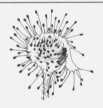

Curving toward the latest prey, the hairs that touch the prey start to release digestive fluid. At the same time, the leaf folds around the prey, so even more hairs can touch the animal.

Now covered with both sticky and digestive juices, the animal quickly dies. The softened portions of the prey are absorbed back into the hairs on the sundew's leaves.

The Indian Pipe

(Monotropa uniflora)

....

location: *temperate regions of the northern hemisphere*

Ghostly white in appearance, the Indian pipe is found growing among the decaying leaves and other dead plant material on the forest floor in damp woods. Unlike some other vampire plants that rob their food directly from host plants, Indian pipes are lazier—they use fungi to steal food for them!

The tiny black seeds of the Indian pipe fall off the plant onto the forest floor. In order to survive, a seed must come in contact with the right fungus, or else the baby Indian pipe will die. These parasites never get very big (less than a foot tall), and they don't live very long. At this time, nobody knows if the Indian pipe hurts the fungus or the plant supplying the fungus with food.

A GRUESOME TWOSOME

....

Time lapse: unknown

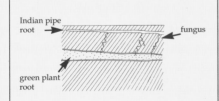

Indian pipe roots join forces with a small, stringy fungus. That fungus stretches underground, connecting to the roots of a green plant that can make its own food.

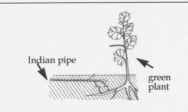

Sugary juices in the green plant's stem and roots are taken away by the fungus, then carried to the roots of the Indian pipe.

The Indian pipe then uses the sugary food to grow. When mature, the plant's flower blooms, and tiny seeds develop, beginning the process again.

The Trumpet Pitcher Plant

Found in very wet places with spongy ground, the bizarre trumpet pitcher plant has "pitcher traps," which are funnel-shaped leaves that look like—you guessed it!—a narrow pitcher. Each plant has two to several of these leaves, each of which grows into an insect-eating pitcher trap. Depending on the type of plant, the traps range in size from just a few inches to almost three feet long.

Like a showy flower, the mouth of each pitcher is brightly colored. Inside the mouth are veins of color, as well as drops of sweet-smelling nectar that lead to a deadly nectar pool below. Enchanted by the pitcher's appearance and scent, a passing fly enters the pitcher . . . never to be seen again.

MEALTIME!

•••••••••••••••••••••••••••••••••••••••

Time lapse: 2 to 5 days

Attracted to the plant's colors and smell, the unsuspecting visitor heads into the pitcher.

Special hairs and slippery wax inside the pitcher cause the prey animal to quickly lose control and tumble into the nectar pool.

There, the animal soon drowns and is digested by a sea of digestive juices, leaving behind only its exoskeleton and wings.

The Rafflesia

THE WORLD'S BIGGEST FLOWER

Time lapse: 2 years

Flies visit the rafflesia to pollinate it. Then the queen of parasites forms seeds. In order to grow, a seed must fall on another grape root—probably by way of an animal.

The seed sprouts and begins feeding on the sugary juices of the grape root.

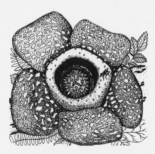

Later, a flower bud forms, then out pops the world's biggest flower!

(Rafflesia)

location: *Sumatra*

Hiding in the faraway jungles of Sumatra is a plant so weird that it almost can't be described. Living off a thin root of a wild grape plant, the rafflesia can grow to a monstrous size—nearly three feet across! Although the rafflesia takes a full two years to prepare to bloom, a mature rafflesia blooms only a few days before rotting in the tropical heat.

Lacking any leaves, stems, or roots for making its own food, this queen of parasites lives entirely on the roots of wild grapes. It is not known if this parasite harms the host grape plant. The enormous flower has an odor similar to some kinds of pitcher plants. This odor attracts flies, which will not be eaten, but rather used to pollinate, or fertilize, the rafflesia.

The Bladderwort

(*Utricularia*)

location: *almost any lake or pond*

The most common of the carnivorous plants, the bladderwort lives in water and has the most amazing traps of all: special sacks that actually vacuum up their victims. Along this plant's long-branched stems are many small, clear bladders, each less than a quarter of an inch across, and each with a single trap-door. The trapdoors have several trigger hairs that activate the traps when touched.

Bladderworts, which lack both roots and leaves, are the only fish-eating plants known. Besides small fish, prey animals include tiny single-celled animals, water fleas, mosquito larvae, and even tadpoles! Found in almost any lake or pond, bladderworts are also easy to grow in aquariums . . . but be sure to remove any of your favorite small fish, or else! This picture shows you what a bladderwort looks like right after it is pulled out of the water. Find out how to grow your own bladderworts at the back of the book!

A WATERY GRAVE

Time lapse: 2 days

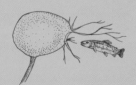

A swimming animal touches one of the trigger hairs, which makes the bladderwort's trapdoor open.

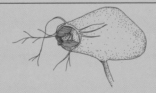

The prey is then sucked into the bladder, and the trapdoor immediately shuts behind it. This process happens at lightning-fast speed—less than 1/500th of a second!

Fluids begin to drip into the bladder, disintegrating the captured animal. The liquid within the bladder is then soaked up, leaving the trap ready for another victim.

The Cobra Lily

THE DEADLY COBRA

Time lapse: 2 to 3 days

Animals are attracted to the nectar on the pitcher and are lured to climb up the tongue toward the nectar drops inside the mouth.

Inside, once the animal tries to escape, it usually can't find its way out because the top of the pitcher has many clear "windows" that look like possible exits.

The confused insect slips and plunges to its death, where it drowns in a pool of nectar.

A lthough the cobra lily is not really a cobra or a lily, it does look like a fearsome snake that is about to attack. Related to the trumpet pitchers, cobra lilies are found in damp, mountainous areas. And like the trumpet pitcher, the cobra lily uses its funnel-shaped leaves to draw in prey animals. However, the cobra lily also has sweet nectar droplets on the outside of its pitcher and a long leafy structure that looks like a long tongue. Curious animals crawl up the interesting tongue, where they soon become lunch for a hungry cobra lily.

The Butterwort

(Pinguicula)

location: *humid environments around the world*

Found in various humid places all over the world, butterworts get their name from the sticky, buttery surface of their leaves. These small killer plants attract flying insects to their greasy, sandpapery leaves not with colors or nectar, but with an irresistible (at least to some flies) fungus-type odor and shiny appearance. Crawling insects may also stroll by only to get stuck on a leaf and later digested! No matter how an insect gets stuck, one thing's for sure: when the butterwort is through with it, only the victim's exoskeleton remains.

A KILLER ENCOUNTER

Time lapse: 2 to 3 days

When an insect lands on the leaf, it becomes stuck.

It soon suffocates from the sticky slime that covers the leaf.

The leaves of butterworts curl around their victim to speed up digestion. When the meal is over, the leaves unfold, and the butterwort lies in wait for its next victim.

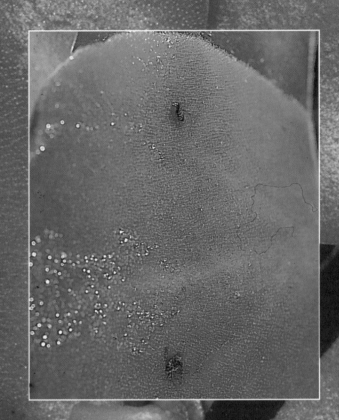

The Golfball Plant

(Pholisma arenarium)

....

location: *southwestern United States, U.S./Mexican border*

Damp forests aren't the only places one can find vampire plants. The relatively rare golfball plant can be found only on coastal and desert sand dunes. During the summer, beautiful golfball-sized heads of purplish flowers appear at ground level in the sand, looking fairly innocent. But underneath the sand lurks the fleshy white stem of this plant, which can reach down more than eight feet to latch onto the roots of neighboring plants. Once attached to the victim's roots, the golfball plant sips the plant's nutritious sugary fluid.

One scientist, who is an expert on golfball plants, thinks that these strange plants may actually *help* their host plants grow bigger. How do they help their hosts? Nobody knows!

MORE THAN A MYSTERY

....

Time lapse: unknown

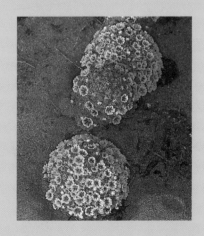

No scientist has been able to learn how a golfball plant spreads its seeds from one plant to another. It's possible that the strong winds blowing across the sand dunes have something to do with moving the golfball plant's seeds to another plant. But no one knows for sure. . . .

The Tropical
Pitcher Plant

(Nepenthes)

location: *Madagascar, Africa, Australia, Indonesia, the Philippines, Malaysia*

While the tropical pitcher plant has pitchers like the trumpet pitcher and the cobra lily, it differs from them, too. How? It is a strong jungle vine that can become gigantic—as long as 50 feet! Not only can each plant have many pitchers, but the pitchers can be huge. The pitchers on the King Monkey Cup, a tropical pitcher plant of the Borneo jungles, can be more than a foot high and half a foot across. That's large enough to take in and consume small reptiles and mammals as large as rats!

The pitchers on these tropical killer plants work much like those of other pitcher plants. Animals are attracted to the pitchers by their bright colors, flowerlike appearance, and the sweet nectar within them.

DON'T GET TOO CLOSE!

Time lapse: about 3 days

An unsuspecting victim heads toward the sweet smell of the nectar inside the pitcher.

Lining the pitcher are waxy flakes that cause the animal to lose its grip on the wall.

Unable to stop itself, the tiny creature falls into the "death" pool below, where it is digested and soaked up by the plant.

The Dodder

(*Cuscuta*)

location: *common throughout most of the world*

Related to morning glories, dodders could be called morning *gories*. Described by ancient Arabs as "plants with the souls of animals," dodders are among the most common vampires of the plant world. A single dodder plant can cover a large tree, and the total length of its branches can reach nearly half a mile!

Some species of dodders have been common pests on both garden and crop plants for centuries. In fact, before this vampire plant was understood, the grape vines hosting the dodder were considered "monstrosities" or even "botanical mistakes" caused by passing comets! Today we know that dodder-infected grape vines are not due to comets, but there is still much we do not know. It is up to future botanists (maybe you?) to solve this and other unsolved mysteries of the plant world!

DESPERATE DODDER

Time lapse: 1 or more years

Dodders have small seeds that sprout in the ground the way normal plant seeds do.

The stem rapidly grows toward a neighboring plant. It then fastens itself to the plant using its piercing haustoria.

The dodder feeds on its host. It can grow thousands of branches, each of which can attack other plants.

Where to See Killer Plants

Hey, don't just sit there and read about killer plants, go find some in their own environment! Although a killer plant may be lurking in your *own* backyard, most are confined to distant or unreachable places like bogs or tropical mountaintops. The best place to start looking for your favorite dangerous plant is at your closest botanical garden or arboretum. Many botanical gardens have living specimens of killer plants, especially carnivorous plants.

Look in your local telephone directory or check out the library to find the arboretum nearest you. Listed below are a few prominent botanical gardens that have killer plants on display. And don't forget to B.Y.O.B. (bring your own bugs)!

Los Angeles County Arboretum
Arcadia, California

Missouri Botanical Garden
St. Louis, Missouri

New York Botanical Garden
Bronx, New York

University of California Botanical Garden
Berkeley, California

You may even want to join the International Carnivorous Plant Society. Send the ICPS a letter today!

The International Carnivorous Plant Society
The Fullerton Arboretum
Department of Biology
California State University
Fullerton, CA 92634